T0078151

Brilliant! In simple, yet profound words, Peggy makes the case for living holy and how to do so. This is a book for all of God's people for all times. Teach this to our children, youth, men and women. This is what the church needs today. This practical and concise book on holiness can be used in Bible study, in the pulpit, for preaching and for teaching. Peggy hit the nail on the head. Get this book!

Bishop John I. Cline, Senior Pastor
New Life Baptist Church,
Tortola, BVI

How to Live Holy

PEGGY CALLENDER CLYNE

WESTBOW
PRESS®
A DIVISION OF THOMAS NELSON
& ZONDERVAN

Scripture taken from the New King James Version. Copyright © 1979, 1980,
1982 by Thomas Nelson, inc. Used by permission. All rights reserved.

Scripture taken from the King James Version of the Bible.

Scripture taken from the Holy Bible, NEW INTERNATIONAL VERSION®.
Copyright © 1973, 1978, 1984 by Biblica, Inc. All rights reserved worldwide.
Used by permission. NEW INTERNATIONAL VERSION® and NIV® are
registered trademarks of Biblica, Inc. Use of either trademark for the offering
of goods or services requires the prior written consent of Biblica US, Inc.

Scripture taken from the Holman Christian Standard Bible ® Copyright ©
2003, 2002, 2000, 1999 by Holman Bible Publishers. All rights reserved.

WestBow Press books may be ordered through booksellers or by contacting:

WestBow Press
A Division of Thomas Nelson & Zondervan
1663 Liberty Drive
Bloomington, IN 47403
www.westbowpress.com
1 (866) 928-1240

ISBN: 978-1-5127-0153-1 (sc)
ISBN: 978-1-5127-0154-8 (e)

Print information available on the last page.

WestBow Press rev. date: 11/17/2015

In memory of Sylvia Rose Marie Williams Mitchell,
whose life epitomized holiness.

Contents

FOREWORD

I grew up in an era of the church (the Pentecostal church) when messages and songs centered around subjects such as heaven, hell, giving your heart to the Lord right now, being saved and sanctified, and holiness or hell. These messages were given with conviction and a sense of urgency to prepare people for what was believed as the very soon coming of the Lord. Altar calls were distinct and frequent with emphasis on "if you were to die tonight, where would you spend eternity?"

Some walked around with a pious attitude, border lining a self-righteous spirit; wearing what they thought was a badge of honor. Looking back on those times, and what culture had begun to shape as the world's view regarding "free love, getting high, and involvement in wars," that specific teaching was really about separation. The scripture declares, "How can light and darkness dwell together?" Without proper discernment and spiritual maturity, such can be the fuel for an elitist mindset; one being more superior than the other.

When we look at the life of Jesus, we observe He shocked the world by His approach, message, and intent. Jesus challenged the religious crowd of His day by appearing with, being seen with, and ministering to some of the very individuals that most thought were not worthy of His time, His effort, and His forgiveness. Jesus didn't wear holiness as a badge of separation. He offered it as a garment that could be worn by all. His teachings were pure, simple, yet piercing. Holiness is a higher standard. It is the personality of God Himself. Holiness is the essence of His nature.

Looking back over the years, I have heard teachings on the subject of holiness with descriptives where the bar was raised so high that very few, including the ones describing it, could obtain or even live it out themselves. Holiness is a way of life that can be lived on a daily basis even in this current maze of blended culture where it seems the lines are not clearly drawn.

The Old Testament states "there was a time when there was no king, no pattern." The result was that every man did what was right in his own eyes. Holiness is not lived from without, but rather from within; as seen in the decisions of an individual who has been inspired by the life of Christ and demonstrated in how they live, treat their families, or conduct business. Holiness is not owned by any particular denomination, sect, or group. Through a relationship with the Holy Spirit, with Him being the guide and the teacher, it is possible that every human being on the planet could understand what it means to be holy.

To be like Christ should be our ultimate goal in life, and through Him we have access into His heart to know His ways, and to exude His essence. Herein I believe is man's greatest discovery.

In covenant with you,
Bishop Joseph A. McCargo
Senior Pastor and Founder
City of Hope IWC, Columbia, MD

ACKNOWLEDGMENTS

I thank God, the Holy Spirit, for His inspiration and patience with me.

I thank my husband, Freddie, and my family for their love and encouragement.

Thank you, Bishop Cline, for your endorsement and for your ideas as I wrote the book's first draft, and thank you for pouring out your soul in the many sermons you preach, especially "God Has His Hand on Me" and "God Expects More." I am a better person because you said yes to God.

Thank you, Bishop McCargo, for taking time to write the Foreword. Thank you for speaking into my life through the years. I think I finally understand your sermon about the importance of "God's timing."

Thank you, Marlene LeFever and Johanna Fisher, for your encouragement and for your friendship, which has withstood the test of time.

And thanks to all of you who supported my desire to write this book. Your kind words and, most importantly, your fervent prayers are sincerely appreciated. Special thanks to the Prayer Warriors at New Life Baptist Church in Tortola, who placed their hands on the manuscript as they prayed. And special thanks to Jacqueline Nathaniel and Joanna Gaskin for their invaluable assistance with content editing. God bless you!

INTRODUCTION

After attending church for more than fifty years, I've concluded that many Christian people are in the dark regarding how to live holy. We really need help. We have a manual, the Holy Bible, that instructs us how to live holy (2 Timothy 3:16), but we often do the exact opposite of what the Word of God teaches: we speak love while harboring hate, we speak oneness while causing discord, and we speak purity while drowning in iniquity. If you ask Christian people why we act that way, we may say that no one is perfect and that we all fall short. We know that "holiness" is a position we have in Jesus, but how to live it out ourselves eludes us. What is "holiness," and why do we find it so challenging?

Holiness can be defined as godliness, consecration, and sanctification, the last of which refers to being set apart for God's use. Holiness is spiritual maturity, the lifestyle God expects from the people who say they have a relationship with Him and who frequent His house, the church.

How to Live Holy encourages readers to consider and implement seven principles that can help us live a more consecrated and mature Christian life. The first principle is *desire*, a *holy hunger* for a deeper relationship with God that results in wanting to please Him (and not ourselves). Desire is a prerequisite for living holy. The second principle is *devotions*, a *holy habit*. These quiet times with God can strengthen our relationship with Him and prepare us to interact with the world. The third principle is *dedication*, the *holy honor* to God that manifests itself in love. God is love, so loving others is a part of living holy. The fourth principle is *denying self*, a *holy handicap* or a self-imposed limitation that recognizes that we must die to ourselves in order to live holy unto the Lord. The fifth principle is *denouncing and detaching*, the *holy hatchet* that identifies evil and cuts off whatever would hinder our goal to live holy. The sixth principle is *declaration*, the *holy heralding* whereby we speak out with authority our case and intention to live holy. The seventh and final principle is *deployment*, the "who" and "what" we summon for *holy help* in order to defeat the Enemy and experience victory.

Is holiness all that serious? I believe it is! We make plans for everything else. Why not have a strategy for living holy, a *modus operandi*, if you will?

> No discipline seems enjoyable at the time,
> but painful. Later on, however, it yields the
> fruit of peace and righteousness to those

who have been trained by it. Therefore strengthen your tired hands and weakened knees, and make straight paths for your feet, so that what is lame may not be dislocated but healed instead.

Pursue peace with everyone, and holiness—without it no one will see the Lord. (Hebrews 12:11–14 HCSB)

May God bless this book for His glory.

Chapter 1

Desire: *Holy Hunger*

Have you ever done anything with excellence that you really did not want to do? In order to please God, you must *want* to please God. Psalm 63:1 (KJV) says, "my soul thirsteth for thee, my flesh longeth for thee in a dry and thirsty land, where no water is." Psalm 1:2 says the blessed man delights in God's law. Psalm 40:8a (NKJV) says, "I delight to do Your will, O my God." Thirsting, longing, delighting: that's desire.

Desire is a yearning. David said, "As the deer pants for streams of water, so my soul pants for you, my God. My soul thirsts for God, for the living God. When can I go and meet with God?" (Psalm 42:1–2 NIV). Jesus admonished us to hunger and thirst after righteousness (Matthew 5:6). That's the kind of desire we need in order to live holy. Desire is a mind-set. If our mind-set is to live holy, then we will desire God. We will recognize that delighting ourselves in Him will result in a holy lifestyle. We'll find ourselves asking God what will please Him.

Therefore, unless Christian people deepen their desire for holiness, their struggle will continue. Consider our typical desires: We desire God's patience and plead, Lord, have mercy on me. We desire God's protection and say, Lord, build a hedge all around me. We desire God's provision and ask, Lord, supply all my needs. However, on a day-to-day, moment-by-moment basis, how often do we desire God's *presence and pray,* Lord, draw me nearer. Sometimes we are so caught up with our selves that thirsting after God isn't even on our minds. What's on our minds? We are. It's all about us! How in the world can we desire someone who's not on our minds? Still, we know that a desire for God's presence is what we need to live holy.

In order to get God on our minds and keep Him there, I suggest we start with daily devotions.

CHAPTER 2

Devotions: *Holy Habit*

Having a daily quiet time with God, preferably first thing in the morning, sets the atmosphere for God's presence. Seek God *before* breakfast: let communion with Him be our first food. Seek him *before* going to work: let fellowship with Him be our first duty. We must seek God before the trials and stresses of the day distract us. The psalmist wrote, "O God, thou art my God; early will I seek thee" (Psalm 63:1a KJV). He affirmed that God was *his* God. In *The Treasury of David*, Charles H. Spurgeon, the highly acclaimed 19ᵗʰ century preacher said, "Possession breeds desire". So if we Christian people say we belong to God, we should desire to seek Him "early".

Mark 1:35 (NIV) makes clear that Jesus also sought His Father "early": "Very early in the morning, while it was still dark, Jesus got up, left the house and went off to a solitary place, where he prayed."

Isaiah, the prophet, wrote, "With my soul have I desired thee in the night; yea, with my spirit within me will I seek thee early: for when thy judgments are in the earth, the inhabitants of the world will learn righteousness" (Isaiah 26:9 KJV).

Following these examples every day can help us to live holy by carrying God's presence into the workplace, the schoolroom—wherever we are. Isaiah's early meeting with God benefited not only him but others as well. Because Isaiah had spent time with God, he had something to share with "the inhabitants of the world" (Isaiah 26:9 KJV). If we have spent time with God, we will have something to meditate on throughout the day and to share with others.

The psalmist wrote that the blessed man meditates on God's Word (Psalm 1:2) day and night. David was a shepherd and the word "meditate" is a pastoral word. It is similar to the words regurgitate and ruminate. This is what sheep do when they chew their cud. They chew their food, store it in one of their stomach's four compartments, rest a while, and return the food to their mouths to chew and continue the process of regurgitation.

But we can only regurgitate what we have eaten. God's word is the Christian's spiritual food and I encourage Christian people to develop the holy habit of daily devotions. "My soul shall be satisfied as with marrow and fatness, writes the psalmist, "and my mouth shall praise thee with joyful lips" (Psalm 63:5 KJV).

4

CHAPTER 3

Dedication: *Holy Honor*

Dedication is commitment and perseverance, so it is continuous desire, sustained desire. Dedication to God and holy living is nonstop and unrelenting.

I think this may be the area in which we Christian people struggle the most. Our dedication is not sustained, which is an oxymoron because, if dedication is "sustained desire," there can be no such thing as unsustained dedication. Dedication implies devotion. (There's that word again.) Other synonyms for *dedication* are *love* and *loyalty*, but Christian people often go from giving God high praise, singing songs about holiness to mistreating our brothers and sisters in Christ. Sometimes I'm not even sure that we equate mistreating our brethren with offending the Lord. Our manual, the Holy Bible, clearly states how we are to treat each other:

> Give to everyone what you owe them: If you owe taxes, pay taxes; if revenue, then revenue; if respect, then respect; if honor, then honor. Let no debt remain outstanding, except the continuing debt to love one another, for whoever loves others has fulfilled the law. The commandments, "You shall not commit adultery," "You shall not murder," "You shall not steal," "You shall not covet," and whatever other command there may be, are summed up in this one command: "Love your neighbor as yourself." Love does no harm to a neighbor. Therefore love is the fulfillment of the law. (Romans 13:7–10 NIV)

Dedication to God and holiness means loving others. We have to remember who we are and to Whom we belong. If we are Christian people in the true sense of the word—the body of Christ—then we belong to God and we represent His kingdom. In days gone by, loyal subjects died for their king. King Jesus asked us only to "love one another." He went on to say, "By this everyone will know that you are my disciples, if you love one another" (John 13:35 NIV). The apostle John almost makes me cringe because he claimed, "Whoever does not love does not know God, because God is love" (1 John 4:8 NIV). Loving others is proof that we know God! Love is greater than faith and hope (1 Corinthians 13:13). Loving others is evidence that we have picked up our cross and followed

Christ's example. Loving others illustrates what Jesus did for us at Calvary.

"Then [Jesus] said to them all: 'Whoever wants to be my disciple must deny themselves and take up their cross daily and follow me'" (Luke 9:23 NIV).

CHAPTER 4

Denying Self: *Holy Handicap*

I am convinced that Jesus' advice in Luke 9:23 to deny ourselves and take up our crosses daily did not just mean to take up our burdens or trials but also to take up death: death to selfish ambitions, death to defiant wills, death to whatever hinders us from following Him totally. In the first chapter of this book I said that Christian people often do the exact opposite of what our manual, the Holy Bible, teaches. One such "opposite" is allowing our flesh to dictate our behavior when God specifically asks us to die to self.

Galatians 2:20 (NKJV) says, "I have been crucified with Christ; it is no longer I who live, but Christ lives in me; and the life which I now live in the flesh I live by faith in the Son of God, who loved me and gave Himself for me." In Colossians 3:3 (NKJV) we read, "For you died, and your life is hidden with Christ in God." Second Corinthians 5:15 (NKJV) tells us, "and He died for all, that those who live should live no longer for themselves, but for Him who died for them and rose again."

In an age of self-empowerment, where so much emphasis is placed on personal achievement and success, the thought of denying ourselves can be unpopular and uncomfortable. Most of us have the ability to get what we want, and we frown upon the idea of doing without. This mind-set creeps into our spiritual lives, causing us not to want even God to tell us what we can and cannot do, yet self-denial is what God requires of us if we are serious about being His disciples and living holy.

Self-denial assumes we choose God's will above our own will. In *Experiencing God*, Henry Blackaby speaks of "adjusting our life to God," stating, "You cannot stay where you are and go with God" (p. 127). He reminds us that even God's Son had to make major adjustments: "For you know the grace of our Lord Jesus Christ, that though He was rich, yet for your sakes He became poor, that you through His poverty might become rich" (2 Corinthians 8:9 NKJV). Also consider Matthew 8:20, which tells us that Jesus said, "Foxes have holes and birds of the air have nests, but the Son of Man has no place to lay his head."

In *The Glory of God*, author Guillermo Maldonado calls Jesus' death on the cross the zenith of all His self-denial. Similarly, we must deny ourselves to say "no" to our rebellious, sinful nature. When the ego says, "I want," we respond, "No." What the ego thinks or feels is not important. The important thing is what our heavenly Father wants us to do. We cannot negotiate with the ego. It must be executed. It must die so that Jesus can live through us! (p. 97)

We are "ambassadors for Christ" (2 Corinthians 5:20). An ambassador denies himself in order to represent his country. He has no other agenda: He gives up his home to go abroad. He gives up comfort and conveniences. In some instances, he gives up family and familiarity because, at least for a time, he is "married" to his country. What have *we* given up lately in order to live holy and represent *our* King? How often do we Christian people deny ourselves and declare death to the flesh?

CHAPTER 5

Denouncing and Detaching: *Holy Hatchet*

"Denouncing" and "detaching" are two words that are closely related to self-denial. Denouncing refers to deploring or condemning, taking a public stand against an evil or something that is wrong, speaking out against it. Detaching is to separate oneself from something, to cut it off.

Christian people who are *serious* about living holy want to mature spiritually and are dedicated to putting Christ and His teachings before their own philosophies. However, Christian people struggle because we fail to "denounce and detach" on a regular basis. As much "Word" as we hear and as many songs as we sing, we still hold on to the flesh. Yes, I know we live in the flesh—we're human; we have a sinful nature—but we often use that as an excuse for not growing up in God the way we could.

The Bible is replete with instructions and encouragements for consistent godly living, and these instructions can become mind-sets when we allow them to. As we spend more time in God's word, our desire to please Him deepens. Will we ever be perfect in this life? Of course not, but we can be better—much better! When we make it our business to agree with God's word, we are less likely to agree with the world's "word" and more likely to put on the whole armor of God (Ephesians 6:10–18) and stand against the Enemy.

Sometimes we are slow to denounce the Enemy's schemes, especially if his suggestions are popular and commonplace, but until we speak out against his tricks, we will see no need to detach ourselves from his influence. The Enemy tries to win our allegiance, so we must get to the place in our lives where we hate his evil ways, resist him, and attach our affection to God. The Holy Spirit is ever present to help us denounce the wisdom of the world and detach ourselves from unholy alliances: "And do not be conformed to this world, but be transformed by the renewing of your mind, that you may prove what *is* that good and acceptable and perfect will of God" (Romans 12:2 NKJV). It's a spiritual mind-set.

To what do you listen? To whom do you listen? What do you watch? Where do you go? John 6:63 (NKJV) tells us that Jesus said, "It is the Spirit who gives life; the flesh profits nothing. The words that I speak to you are spirit, and *they* are life". When we *denounce* evil and *detach* ourselves from it, we are free to attach ourselves to the Spirit, who gives life. Destructive mind-sets invade our mind less often when we agree with God more often.

However, just as we can't agree with someone if we don't know what the person has said, we can't agree with God if we haven't read and heard His word. We must know what He says and desire to obey Him rather than man (Acts 5:29).

Chapter 6

Declaration: *Holy Heralding*

To declare is to say publicly, state, announce, speak out, proclaim, speak with emphasis and authority.

When we are *serious* about wanting to live holy, we declare holiness! Instead of declaring, "I'm my own person; don't tell me how to live," and other affirmations rooted in self-centeredness, we declare, "I belong to God, I've been bought with a price, I am NOT my own, I glorify God in my body and my spirit, which are God's" (1 Corinthians 6:19–20, emphasis mine); "My members are instruments of righteousness unto God" (Romans 6:13); and "My heart has been sprinkled from an evil conscience" (Hebrews 10:22). In fact, "before the creation of the world, I was chosen by the Father to be holy and blameless in His sight" (Ephesians 1:4).

When we are *serious* about wanting to live holy, we declare death to the flesh: "I have been crucified with

Christ" (Galatians 2:20); "My sinful nature with its passions and desires has been crucified" (Galatians 5:24); and "I am no longer a slave to sin" (Romans 6:6).

When we are *serious* about holiness, we declare our victories: "And they overcame him by the blood of the Lamb, and by the word of their testimony; and they loved not their lives unto the death" (Revelation 12:11); "I am redeemed by the LORD: I have been redeemed from the hand of the enemy" (Psalm 107:2); and "I submit [surrender] to God; I resist the devil and he flees from me" (James 4:7).

When we are *serious* about holiness, we declare our privileges: "I have boldness to enter into the presence of God" (Hebrews 10:19); "I have a High Priest Who intercedes for me" (Hebrews 10:20); and "I am a living stone; a chosen race, a royal priesthood, a holy nation. I am a person for God's own possession. He has called me out of darkness into His marvelous light. I have received God's mercy" (1 Peter 2:4–10).

When said regularly and emphatically *by faith*, declarations like these will help us to live holy. We can even print them out, along with other Bible verses, to use as visual reminders like those that God suggested for the Israelites:

> And you shall have the tassel, that you may look upon it and remember all the

commandments of the Lord and do them,
and that you *may* not follow the harlotry to
which your own heart and your own eyes
are inclined, and that you may remember
and do all My commandments, and be holy
for your God. (Numbers 15:39–40 NKJV)

My pastor said, "Your life is at the mercy of your mouth,"
as there is a connection between the words we speak and
our life. Proverbs 13:3 warns us to "guard" our mouths in
order to "preserve" our lives. Holy declarations can help
those who are serious about living holy lives.

CHAPTER 7

Deployment: *Holy Help*

What does "deployment" mean? *Webster's New Collegiate Dictionary* (1960) defines it as extending the front and reducing the depth of something. A similar, but more modern definition is "to form an extended front or *line*; to arrange in a position of readiness, or to move strategically or appropriately" (www.dictionary.com).

When we are *serious* about living holy, we recognize we are in a war, a spiritual battle. My pastor says, "We have a real Enemy." Whenever there's the Enemy, there's also the need for a strategy, a plan to defeat the Enemy. After we "suit up" in our armor (Ephesians 6:12–17), we're ready for battle. Our plan for holy living includes the living Word of God (Jesus), the written Word of God (the Bible), the Holy Spirit, prayer, and God's people (the church).

Let us visualize Jesus, the living Word of God, at the right hand of the Father, interceding for us (Romans

8:34). Imagine Him asking the Father to help us to stay focused and "hold firmly to the faith we profess" (Hebrews 4:14). Imagine Him pleading with our Father for us to be one, just as He and His Father are one (John 17:22). Imagine Jesus pointing to the scars He still bears as a result of His sacrifice for us at Calvary and asking the Father to forgive us — over and over again. Imagine, if you can, an actual bloodline spread out in the shape of a mighty fortress, strategically positioned to shield us from the Enemy, Jesus, our strong tower! (Psalm 61:3).

Let us visualize spreading out the written Word of God in an extended front line. Among the verses are those that we declared in the previous chapter 6. As we spread out the Scripture verses, we remember that the Word is our sword (Ephesians 6:17) and that it is powerful and sharp (Hebrews 4:12).

While doing battle, we remember the Person of the Holy Spirit. He's harder to visualize than Jesus and the written Word are, but we know He's there! He is part of that extended front that wars against the Enemy on our behalf. When the battle gets hot and we're almost ready to give up, we recall Romans 8:26–27 (NKJV): "Likewise the Spirit also helps in our weaknesses. For we do not know what we should pray for as we ought, but the Spirit Himself makes intercession for us with groanings which cannot be uttered. Now He who searches the hearts knows what the mind of the Spirit *is,* because

He makes intercession for the saints according to *the will of* God."

With that assurance, let's visualize a prayer line with prayers woven together and intertwined with the Scripture verses, agreeing with God's Word and pleading the blood of Jesus. We can begin with the declaration verses in chapter 6 and add to our arsenal. The more ammunition we have from our manual, the better our position to win the battle against the Enemy!

Visualize the woven prayer lines being spread out by God's praying people. See us linked together arm in arm, praying for victory over our mutual Enemy. Let us visualize the love and unity we have in the Holy Spirit. These are our brothers and sisters in Christ, who are a part of that extended front, arranged in positions of readiness. There is not a chance of friendly fire among us. Picture us in your mind, moving forward strategically with a plan of action to defeat the Enemy.

We are not alone in the fight. We have the Father, the Son and the Holy Spirit. We have the Bible, God's Holy Word. We have prayer and the power it brings. We have God's people, the church. Love and fellowship were a vital aspect of the early church; my pastor often mentions the importance of love among the brethren and calls the fellowship ministries in our church "life net groups." When a person accepts Jesus Christ as Savior and Lord, he or she is encouraged to join a life net group, which is structured to help the person mature in the Lord.

We are positioned for victory! With a sincere *desire* for God's presence, nurtured with daily *devotions*, persistent *dedication*, *self-denial*, *denouncing* worldliness and *detaching* ourselves from it, and with a mind-set to *declare* our position in Christ and *deploy* our "troops," we can live holy!

Summary and Strategies

Chapter 1—Desire

Summary: Desire is thirsting, longing, and delighting. It's a hungering-after.

Strategies:

Ask yourself:

- How can I acquire a desire for God? (Brainstorm some answers.)
- Who or what do I desire? Why?
- Is there a pattern for the people or things for which I find myself thirsting?

Tell yourself:

- I will spend more time with the Lover of my soul.
- I will spend less time pleasing myself and others.

Suggested Reading:

A. W. Tozer, *The Pursuit of God*
Tommy Tenney, *The God Chasers*

Summary and Strategies

Chapter 2—Devotions

Summary: Devotions are the quiet times we spend with God.

Strategies:

Ask yourself:

- Do I have a *regular* quiet time with God? When? What does it include (e.g., reading His Word, praying, singing, worshipping, "hearing" Him)? How often do I really "meditate"?
- If I don't have regular devotions, what can I do differently in my daily schedule to include them?

Tell yourself:

- What you commit to do regarding devotions.
- How you will evaluate at the end of each day the effectiveness of having had devotions.

Suggested Reading:

L. B. Cowman, *Streams in the Desert*
Oswald Chambers, *My Utmost for His Highest*
RBC Ministries, *Our Daily Bread*

Rick Warren, *The Purpose-Driven Life*

Tim Hughes, *Here Am I To Worship*, a devotional book for
music lovers

Sarah Young, *Jesus Calling: Enjoying Peace in His Presence*

Mary Wilder Tileston, *Joy and Strength*

Tim LaHaye, *How to Study the Bible for Yourself*

Summary and Strategies

Chapter 3—Dedication

Summary: Dedication to God and holy living
manifests itself in love.

Strategies:

Ask yourself:

- In what ways do I sometimes profess to love God
  without loving God's people?
- To what extent would I go to show my love
  for God?
- To what extent would I go to show my love for
  people?

Tell yourself:

- From now on, I will measure my love for God by
  how much I love others.
- From now on, I will make a conscious effort to
  put into practice the songs I sing in church.

Suggested Reading:

Henry Blackaby, *What the Spirit is Saying to the Churches*
Charles Swindoll, *Moses: A Man of Self-Less Dedication*

SUMMARY AND STRATEGIES

Chapter 4—Denying Self

Summary: Self-denial is "dying to self" in order to live for Christ.

Strategies:

Ask yourself:

- What have I "crucified" lately in order to starve my flesh?
- Who can I ask to help me be accountable in my areas of struggle (e.g., food and beverages, unforgiveness, pride, sexual sins, health goals, spiritual lethargy, tithing and other money matters, rebellion/witchcraft, gossip, integrity, productivity, obedience, faith and trust)? Please add your area of struggle if it is not listed here.

Tell yourself:

- I will acknowledge my sin (Psalm 51:3).
- I will repent for having offended God (Psalm 51:4) and allow Him to change me by renewing my mind (Romans 12:2).

Suggested Reading:

Henry Blackaby and Claude King,
    Experiencing God
John Calvin, *Golden Booklet of the True Christian Life*

SUMMARY AND STRATEGIES

Chapter 5—Denouncing and Detaching

Summary: Denouncing is condemning evil; detaching is cutting it off.

Strategies:

Ask yourself:

- Who or what is my holy hatchet?
- How much do the opinions of others influence my decision to live holy?
- What are some things I do and justify that I really should condemn and "kill"?
- What are some things other people do that I wrongfully justify and condone?

Tell yourself:

- I can be right with my culture and wrong with God.
- I will write down and implement at least three strategies for "killing" anything that's trying to "kill" me.
- I will commit to being a spiritual Nathan to whomever God leads me. (See 2 Samuel 12:1-13.)

- I will submit to Godly counsel from whomever God sends.

Suggested Reading:

Beth Moore, *Praying God's Word: Breaking Free from Spiritual Strongholds*

Summary and Strategies

Chapter 6—Declaration

Summary: Holy declarations can be very helpful in living a holy life.

Strategies:

Ask yourself:

- What do I say that hinders my spiritual growth and maturity?
- Why do I sometimes say the opposite of what I want manifested in my life?

Tell yourself:

- I will guard my mouth in order to preserve my life (Proverbs 13:3).
- My body is a tool for God to use for righteousness (Based on Romans 6:13).
- I will be a channel of blessing for others by what I declare *to* them and *about* them.

Suggested Reading:

Cindy Trimm, *Commanding Your Morning*

Summary and Strategies

Chapter 7—Deployment

Summary: Deploying our "troops" helps us be victorious over the Enemy.

Strategies:

Ask yourself:

- On a day-to-day, moment-by-moment basis, do I visualize victory?
- What spiritual gifts do I bring to the body of Christ to equip God's people to live holy?

Tell yourself:

- I am positioned for victory.
- I have "holy help" and I will survive the Enemy's attacks.
- With God's help, I will develop my spiritual gifts for God's glory and for the common good of God's people.

Suggested Reading:

Book of Esther (Old Testament)
The Acts of the Apostles (New Testament)

OH, TO BE WISE AND HOLY

Oh, to be wise and holy, is what I want to be
And to honour my Saviour, through trials come what may
Just to know Jesus is with me, no matter where I go
I will love God forever
I'll bless his name throughout my days

Oh, to be wise and holy, is what God wants of me
I will bless his name forever, though storm clouds pave
the way
I'm so glad Jesus, He loves me, He's with me day by day
I will trust God forever, for He's the One who saves by
grace

My Lord, I bless your name for you are worthy
Oh, Lord, I honour you, Ancient of Days
Just to know that you are with me
And that you're standing by my side

I will go through every storm
I'll make it through every trial
I'll never cease to praise you
I'll never cease to honour you
I'll never cease to love you and abide through all my days

Oh, to be wise and holy, is what God wants of me
I will practice discretion for it will preserve me
I must seek understanding 'cause it will keep me safe...
    so safe
I'll hide his commandments (3x)
For long life and length of days

Oh Lord, I thank you for your tender mercies
My Lord, I worship you sweet El Shaddai
I'm so glad to know that you defend me (yes you do)
You will always be my guide

I will go through every storm
I'll make it through every trial
I'll never cease to praise you
I'll never cease to honour you
I'll never cease to love you and abide
Throughout all my days.

—Donna Clyne-Thomas

AUTHOR BIO

Peggy Clyne is a retired church administrator, self-published author and Christian Education worker. She attended the former Barrington College in Rhode Island, holds a Bachelor of Religious Education Degree (BRE) from the former Northeastern Bible Institute, Essex Fells, NJ, and was a self-supported missionary to St. Thomas, USVI in the l960's. A Christian for more than 50 years, Peggy relates to the struggle of holiness. She hosts ZKING radio's "Building Blocks", short motivational messages with the motto: "We are building a better life one block at a time."

Peggy resides in the British Virgin Islands with her husband, Freddie, and family.

Contact Information

Peggy Clyne

P.O. Box 11156

c/o Rush-It, Inc.

St. Thomas, USVI 00801

Email:	pclyne14@gmail.com
Website:	www.buildingblocksbvi.com
Telephone:	(284) 495-9314
Facebook:	https://www.facebook.com/peggy.clyne

Printed in the United States
By Bookmasters